# The Top 10 Best Practices in Affiliate Marketing

## Internet Primer Series

*By Matt Frary*

SmarterChaos.com Inc.
340 3rd Street
Castle Rock, CO 80104

www.smarterchaos.com

## DISCLAIMER

This booklet has been written to provide information about developing a successful podcast that will impress all who hear it. Every effort has been taken to make this booklet as complete, helpful and accurate as possible.

This booklet is intended to be educational and instructional. The author and/or the publisher do not guarantee that the information contained in this booklet is comprehensive or complete, and will not be responsible for any errors or omissions. The author and/or publisher bear neither liability nor responsibility to any person or entity with respect to any loss or damage caused or alleged to be caused directly or indirectly by the information in this booklet.

# TABLE OF CONTENTS

## ABOUT MATT FRARY

Matt Frary has been involved in online marketing and customer lead generation for over 15 years and is the founder and CEO of SmarterChaos, where he has realized his true potential as the "Chief of Chaos". SmarterChaos is a performance marketing agency that helps advertisers find the right user at the right time on the right media partner's website.

Matt learned the power of affiliate marketing early in his career when he got a job placing advertisements on travel websites for a luggage company. He then moved on to work with a charity mall, managing relationships with companies such as Amazon, eBay and Barnes and Noble.

He has also worked for Microsoft building lead generation channels for automobiles, and did an internship with Mercedes Benz where he created a marketing plan for the launch of their "smart car" in the U.S.

He has managed affiliate networks that turn over tens of millions of dollars per year in revenue, with over 1,600 advertisers and 60,000 affiliates involved.

He has a Bachelor's Degree in marketing and business from the University of Colorado, with concentrations in Russian, finance and brand marketing. He also has an MBA from Thunderbird Graduate School.

Matt is sought after speaker on pay for performance marketing, lead generation and ethical marketing practices. He is also the host of the podcast **Chaos Makes Sense.**

# INTRODUCTION

Hi, my name is Matt Frary and I have found that every Advertiser of every product in the United States, and internationally, asks the same question over and over again: **"What do I need to know to run a successful Affiliate Program?"**

In short, wouldn't it be great to know the *silver bullet* of Affiliate Marketing, and learn from years and years of failures and successes?

Well, I don't know about having a silver bullet, but I do know that **I've failed and succeeded** at affiliate marketing more times than I can count!

To answer this question, I interviewed Jeannine Crooks of **Affiliate Window,** who has also succeeded many times over in this industry. We both agreed on the **Top 10 Best Practices in Affiliate Marketing.**

We've spilt these up into the **Three Keys to Creating a Successful Affiliate Program** and the **Seven Habits of Highly Effective Advertisers.**

# THE 3 KEYS TO CREATING A SUCCESSFUL AFFILIATE PROGRAM

## 1. DEVELOP A BUSINESS PLAN

**Anything worth doing is worth doing right.** There's actually a lot of risk involved in the development of a successful affiliate program – all your investment, all your time. But where there is risk, there is also great reward.

By developing a business plan, you are focusing on what it is you are going to do, and you are making a commitment to it. There are tremendous opportunities to offer, so don't go in without a plan.

You should start off with a new plan each year and review it every quarter. Include things like confirming that everyone's duties are a *good fit* for their skill set, and make sure that someone's *accountable* for each task. Then make sure you monitor how it's going.

It's also important to know your **key performance indicators.**

**Are you reaching your milestones?**

**Do you have the resources you need?**

Your business plan is your roadmap for creating a successful affiliate program.

## 2. CONDUCT A SWOT ANALYSIS

Once you commit to a plan, take a close look at your competition. It's critical to find out as much as you can about them, such as:

**What are their policies?**

**What are their commission rates and coupon policies?**

**How long are their cookies?**

And especially . . .

**Who are they working with that you're not working with?**

Analyzing the competition will reveal where the opportunities are.

**To do this, use the S.W.O.T. framework:**

1. Strengths
2. Weaknesses
3. Opportunities
4. Threats

That way, you'll be starting off by taking a thorough look at everything, and you can find some way to have an advantage that your competitors don't.

For example: if you're commission rate is 4%, and your competitor is offering 7%, then you're going to have an uphill battle.

I like to look beyond what your competitors are **doing right,** and also look at what they are **doing wrong.** This isn't always easy. I recently did a *competitive analysis* of advertisers programs.

We went looking for affiliate programs, but we didn't just look for *live ones,* we looked for *dead ones!*

We wanted to see why they **died,** what their **commission rate** was, who they were **partnered** with, and what kind of **resources** and **support** were they putting into it. You can learn a lot by looking at old affiliate programs that didn't work.

Also, your affiliates can give you great insights into what your competitors are offering that is attractive to them. It's important not to put them on the spot or make them feel awkward, so ask questions like:

**"How can we make our program better?"**

**"What offer from another merchant would make you choose them over us?"**

**"What can we help you with so we can grow together?"**

You need to take into consideration what they say. They will tell you what you could be doing better, and point out the *road blocks* in your program. From there, it's your job as the account manager, or affiliate manager, to remove those *road blocks!*

## 3. BUILD A RELATIONSHIP

The biggest thing to understand is that you're **cultivating** and **nurturing** a relationship. Really get to know your affiliates and find out what extra assistance they need from you. It can mean the difference between somebody choosing you over a competitor. Affiliates and advertisers should both be looking for a good fit.

**I find it really bizarre when merchants auto-approve an affiliate.**

If that's all the attention they're putting into choosing their affiliates, how much attention are they going to pay to motivating them and responding to questions?

It's important to screen every applicant before approving them. A lot of new affiliates try and sign up to every program they can find, even though they aren't really suited to 90% of them! To avoid this, affiliate managers need to make sure applicants are a good match first.

Another advantage of building a close relationship with your affiliates, and knowing their strengths and weaknesses, is you can identify a ton of opportunities. Maybe they are generating a *ton* of clicks, but aren't converting. Together, you might be able to come up with just one little tweak that **sends sales through the roof!**

# 7 HABITS OF HIGHLY EFFECTIVE ADVERTISERS

**Best practices are a two-way street.** Your affiliates are working *hard* to earn traffic and conversions. Advertisers have to play their part too.

**I recommend advertisers use the following best practices when working with affiliates:**

# 1. BE ON THE PROWL FOR NEW AFFILIATES

You always have to be on the lookout for new affiliates. You're probably going to have 25% churn on an annual basis, including probably 10% of your top guys. You constantly have to be **looking for new affiliates to recruit,** and **growing existing affiliates** to take them from the masses, to top performers.

**Set it and forget it is a myth!**

## 2. BE TRANSPARENT

Another thing that's really important is to make sure that your program **terms and policies** are very clear.

That way your affiliates don't have to worry if there is a grey area, thinking, "Can I do this?" Or, "Can I do that?"

Itemize things as much as possible. Make it **easy** for them so they don't have to waste a lot of time tracking you down.

## 3. BE RESPONSIVE TO YOUR AFFILIATES

When an affiliate from one of your affiliate programs does contact you, **answer them!**

We hear a lot of stories, "I e-mailed so-and-so, or I left a voicemail for them, and I never heard back". That's the **worst** thing you can do. If the affiliate took the time to reach out to you, take the time to answer them back.

This is a *relationship*.

Your publishers want that respect of the phone call. They want your respect to give them the right tools, and the right tricks. It's a collaboration – a partnership between your **affiliate manager** and the **affiliate.**

## 4. MAKE IT FUN- FOR EVERYONE

**Make your program fun!** Contests and incentive programs can get affiliates *excited* about your program. That's when they want to play with you, and not somebody else. Getting even one or two affiliates motivated about your program can do *amazing* things to your numbers!

Running a great affiliate program is not difficult, but you do have to work at it. *This doesn't mean, however, that you can't have fun along the way.* I think everybody can make a **good amount of money** doing this; make a nice living, and have a successful program. Sometimes though, we take ourselves *too* seriously, or take something out of context.

**Let's have fun and build programs!**

And shake it up a bit. For example, if you're going to hold a contest, do something that's going to enable **everybody to have a chance at winning,** not just the person with the most sales. You don't want the same guys winning *every single time.*

## 5. EMBRACE CREATIVITY

**This industry has a lot of flexibility.** It's not *rocket science*, but it is an opportunity to be creative. Affiliates are always coming up with fascinating new ways to promote and new ways to present.

The online space is a great place to **let your imagination run wild.** Give your affiliates the freedom to come up with some really fun ways to present things to the consumer and that makes them want to buy.

There is not just one way to do affiliate marketing, and it's difficult to even define what an affiliate is. At the end of the day, it refers to someone who **partners with companies online and makes money on a commission base by driving them customers.** Beyond that, it's a blank canvas!

## 6. WORK YOUR CONTENT

**Content is still king in these programs.** Advertisers need to have their content right. It could be coupons, banners, articles, audio or video.

The affiliate has created a **curated space** online. When the advertiser has the right content to drop into that space, that's the flash play. *That's where you make sales!*

It's amazing what some people create. They make it an enjoyable experience for the customer, and that should always be your main goal.

# 7. KEEP UP WITH WHAT'S HAPPENING

You also have to remember that we're chasing a **moving target.** You have to be aware of what the *hottest* trends in the industry are, and what new changes have been made to the latest Google algorithm.

**Merchants need to be flexible, and adapt to those changes.**

The ones that continue to evolve with their affiliates will grow like crazy. There are so many opportunities out there, especially internationally. If a company that previously only did business in the U.S figures out how to ship their products to places like Europe, Australia and South America, they *can tap into affiliates across the globe!*

And these days there are businesses who are figuring out how to do that. They are expanding and finding new markets, and while this approach isn't possible for everyone, some people are missing out simply because they haven't tried.

**Another exciting opportunity is everything that's happening with mobile.**

More and more, merchants are understanding that you have to have a site that is compatible with mobile devices. The majority of people today view the Internet on their mobile devices, and you need to tap into that.

## FOLLOWING THESE TOP 10 BEST PRACTICES FOR AFFILIATE PROGRAMS MEANS WE CAN MAKE MORE MONEY, CREATE MORE VALUE, AND LIVE THE LIFE WE DREAM OF!

We don't have to make Affiliate Marketing difficult, and we don't have to discover some magical or mythical formula. We just have to follow a few guidelines, and they will get you well on your way to being successful. Affiliate Marketing can sometimes seem chaotic, but at **SmarterChaos: Online Performance Marketing,** we create order from chaos, and we will drive your sales!

340 3rd St
Castle Rock, CO 80104

Website: www.smarterchaos.com
Telephone: (720) 583-1136

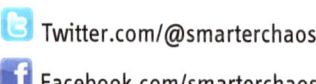 Twitter.com/@smarterchaos
Facebook.com/smarterchaos